A LifeBuilder

JONAH, JOEL & AMOS

12 studies
for individuals or groups

Doug & Doris Haugen

With Notes for Leaders

Getting the Most Out of
Jonah, Joel & Amos

In "The Great Stone Face" Nathaniel Hawthorne told the story of a rock formation that resembled a human face on the side of a mountain. Legend had it that a truly great man resembling the great stone face would someday come to the nearby town. One boy made it his life's goal to study the face and search for its resemblance in others. Over the years he spent countless hours gazing with wonder at that awesome face. As the boy matured into manhood, and as life's influence molded him, those around him were amazed to see what he had become—the great stone face!

A wise professor once said, "What gets your attention, gets you." This is especially true in the books of Jonah, Joel and Amos. In each book God takes drastic measures to get people's attention. He does so not because he delights in calamity but because he desires our fellowship. No matter who we are—prophet, pagan or God's own people—he will do whatever is necessary to draw us to himself.

Jonah

Jonah prophesied in the eighth century B.C., during or shortly before the reign of Jeroboam II (793-753 B.C.). God called him to preach to Nineveh, the capital of Assyria, which was the most powerful nation on earth. The more we know about Assyria, the more we understand why Jonah was reluctant to preach there. The Assyrians were a fierce, warring people who often treated their captives ruthlessly. Jonah had good reason to be afraid!

But fear was not the only thing that made Jonah reluctant. His attitude reflects the racial prejudice common in his day. The "chosen people" could not imagine that God could care about other nations—especially one as vile and idolatrous as Assyria. So the book of Jonah becomes a powerful illustration of the fact that God does not want "anyone to perish, but everyone to come to repentance" (2 Peter 3:9).

The story of Jonah has been the subject of much controversy. Some scholars have rejected its historical validity, preferring to view it as an allegory or parable. However, two things should be noted about this view. First, few people questioned the historicity of Jonah until the nineteenth century, when liberal scholars launched an attack not only on this book but also on every book in the Bible. They objected to its historicity primarily because of the incident of Jonah being swallowed by a fish. However, even from a natural standpoint this incident is quite possible. In his *Introduction to the Old Testament*, R. K. Harrison points out that there are other reliable records of people being swallowed by large fish and surviving.[*]

Second, Jesus himself viewed the story of Jonah as history (Matthew 12:38-41; Luke 11:29-30, 32), comparing it to the greater miracle of his resurrection. Surely those who believe in the latter should have no difficulty believing in the former.

Joel

We know little about the man Joel, other than the fact that his message was geared toward Judah, and he was probably a resident of Jerusalem. The date of his writing is disputed among scholars. While some say Joel prophesied as late as 400 B.C., many believe he was a contemporary of Jonah and Amos.

Joel's prophecy came in the wake of a devastating locust plague. Joel saw this plague as a sign of God's judgment and warned that unless the people returned to the Lord they would face even greater judgment on the day of the Lord. But to those willing to "rend their hearts" he promised great blessings that would more than repay "the years the locusts have eaten" (2:25).

Amos

Although Amos was a farmer from Judah, he prophesied to Israel, the

---

[*]R. K. Harrison, *Introduction to the Old Testament* (Grand Rapids, Mich.: Eerdmans, 1969), pp. 907-8.

Northern Kingdom, around 760 B.C. During this period the nation was secure and the upper classes prospered. Archaeological discoveries at Megiddo and Samaria have uncovered carved ivory inlays that were used in the furniture and decorative paneling in the homes of the wealthy. But instead of using their wealth to serve the needy, the upper classes were deaf to their cries. In fact, the wealthy maintained their lifestyle by oppressing the poor.

Although the Israelites continued to worship God, their worship was cold and self-serving. Jeroboam had built temples in Bethel and Dan so the people would worship in the north rather than traveling to Jerusalem. But God viewed this worship as idolatrous and declared, "I hate, I despise your religious feasts; I cannot stand your assemblies. Even though you bring me burnt offerings and grain offerings, I will not accept them" (Amos 5:21-22).

God's judgment came against Israel in the form of famine, drought and plagues. But because the people failed to return to the Lord, Amos prophesied that all but a remnant would be destroyed. Still the Lord pleaded with Israel, "Seek good, not evil, that you may live!" (Amos 5:14).

The books of Jonah, Joel and Amos have a powerful message today. We sometimes run from God's will and need to be brought back. At other times we wander from God's ways and need to return to him. And we often seek the wrong things, forgetting the One who is the only source of true life. These prophets challenge us to forsake anything and everything that hinders our relationship with God. Together they proclaim, "Seek the Lord and live!"

Suggestions for Individual Study

1. As you begin each study, pray that God will speak to you through his Word.

2. Read the introduction to the study and respond to the personal reflection question or exercise. This is designed to help you focus on God and on the theme of the study.

3. Each study deals with a particular passage—so that you can delve into the author's meaning in that context. Read and reread the passage to be studied. The questions are written using the language of the New International Version, so you may wish to use that version of the Bible. The New Revised Standard Version is also recommended.

4. This is an inductive Bible study, designed to help you discover for yourself what Scripture is saying. The study includes three types of questions. *Observation* questions ask about the basic facts: who, what, when, where and how. *Interpretation* questions delve into the meaning of the passage. *Application* questions help you discover the implications of the text for growing in Christ. These three keys unlock the treasures of Scripture.

Write your answers to the questions in the spaces provided or in a personal journal. Writing can bring clarity and deeper understanding of yourself and of God's Word.

5. It might be good to have a Bible dictionary handy. Use it to look up any unfamiliar words, names or places.

6. Use the prayer suggestion to guide you in thanking God for what you have learned and to pray about the applications that have come to mind.

7. You may want to go on to the suggestion under "Now or Later," or you may want to use that idea for your next study.

Suggestions for Members of a Group Study

1. Come to the study prepared. Follow the suggestions for individual study mentioned above. You will find that careful preparation will greatly enrich your time spent in group discussion.

2. Be willing to participate in the discussion. The leader of your group will not be lecturing. Instead, he or she will be encouraging the members of the group to discuss what they have learned. The leader will be asking the questions that are found in this guide.

3. Stick to the topic being discussed. Your answers should be based on the verses which are the focus of the discussion and not on outside authorities such as commentaries or speakers. These studies focus on a particular passage of Scripture. Only rarely should you refer to other portions of the Bible. This allows for everyone to participate in in-depth study on equal ground.

4. Be sensitive to the other members of the group. Listen attentively when they describe what they have learned. You may be surprised by their insights! Each question assumes a variety of answers. Many questions do not have "right" answers, particularly questions that aim at meaning or application. Instead the questions push us to explore the passage more thoroughly.

When possible, link what you say to the comments of others. Also, be affirming whenever you can. This will encourage some of the more hesitant members of the group to participate.

5. Be careful not to dominate the discussion. We are sometimes so eager to express our thoughts that we leave too little opportunity for others to respond. By all means participate! But allow others to also.

6. Expect God to teach you through the passage being discussed and through the other members of the group. Pray that you will have an enjoyable and profitable time together, but also that as a result of the study you will find ways that you can take action individually and/or as a group.

7. Remember that anything said in the group is considered confidential and should not be discussed outside the group unless specific permission is given to do so.

8. If you are the group leader, you will find additional suggestions at the back of the guide.

1

Jonah's Disobedience and Prayer

Jonah 1—2

Don't hit your sister! Sometimes it takes all the willpower we have as children to obey. As adults we may have an approach-avoidance response to God's will for our lives. We may intentionally seek spiritual growth and fulfillment, yet withdraw or pull back when God's call conflicts with "our vision" for the future.

GROUP DISCUSSION. When you were a child, how was your disobedience sometimes more costly than obedience?

PERSONAL REFLECTION. When have you been in the position of doing right or wrong, that is, following what you believed to be God's will for you or not? Jonah attempted to run as far as possible from God. Most of us are more subtle than that. How have you run from God?

I Kings 14 24-27 (page 8)

Nineveh was the capital of Assyria, a nation that was a fierce and powerful enemy of Israel to the northeast. *Read Jonah 1—2.*

1. From this text what do you discover about what Jonah is like?

---

2. Tarshish, traditionally identified as Spain, was over two thousand miles in the opposite direction of Nineveh. While Jonah was journeying to Tarshish, what kinds of thoughts and feelings might he have experienced?

---

3. Where is the last place you would want to be a witness and why?

---

4. How is Jonah's response to the storm (1:5) different from that of the sailors?

---

5. After hearing Jonah's suggestion, what new tensions and struggles do the sailors experience (1:12-14)?

P2L4

---

6. In what ways does God use this calamity to demonstrate his grace and mercy (1:15-17)?

7. How does this chapter illustrate the futility of running from God?

8. Describe a situation in which you felt like you were physically, emotionally or spiritually in a deep, dark pit (2:6). How did the Lord provide for you?

9. What was Jonah's condition when he finally remembered to pray (2:1-2, 7)?

10. How could Jonah pray a prayer of thanksgiving from the belly of a whale?

Why do you think we sometimes have to sink so low before we remember God?

11. What do you think Jonah learned through this experience?

12. What has God taught you through disobedience?

Take time to identify experiences of God's discipline and grace in your life. Quietly reaffirm your commitment to obey him.

Now or Later

Describe various ways that God has used to get your attention to follow him. What were the results? Write a prayer of thanksgiving.

2

Jonah's Obedience

Jonah 3

Great revivals have occurred throughout history—among the Jews in the first century, the tribes of Ireland in the fifth century, the Protestants in the sixteenth century and the people of Wales in the twentieth century. Yet one of the greatest revivals of all time occurred hundreds of years before any of these—the amazing revival in Nineveh described in Jonah.

GROUP DISCUSSION. Sackcloth and ashes were symbols of repentance and revival. If a genuine turning to God were to occur in this country, what signs would you expect to see?

PERSONAL REFLECTION. What person or group would you struggle to share God's message with? Why? Take a moment for confession and ask for God's help.

In this chapter we'll see the results of Jonah's obedience. *Read Jonah 3.*

1. If you were Jonah, how would you have felt when the word of the Lord came to you a second time (vv. 1-2)?

2. How did the Ninevites respond to Jonah's proclamation, "Forty more days and Nineveh will be overturned!" (v. 4)?

3. Nineveh was a city in Assyria, one of the most powerful nations on earth, known especially for its military might and brutality. How would this make it difficult for Jonah to be obedient?

4. What evidence is there that the Ninevites were sincere in their repentance (vv. 5-9)?

5. Verse 4 says Jonah "proclaimed." Verse 5 says the Ninevites "believed God." After all of Jonah's running and rebellion, how could it be so easy?

6. How and why does the Lord respond to the Ninevites (v. 10)?

7. What view of God do the Ninevites express in this chapter?

_____

8. How does our view of God affect our willingness to turn away from our sins and turn toward God?

_____

9. Describe one area in your life where you feel a need for repentance.

_____

10. What actions can you take to demonstrate the sincerity of your repentance?

Spend some time before the Lord expressing your repentance and experiencing God's grace.

Now or Later
Describe a situation in which you found it difficult to share the gospel with someone. Why was it difficult? How can these kinds of difficulties be overcome?

3

Jonah's Anger

Jonah 4

Animosities between individuals and groups of people are a given in our world today. Just take a look at the headlines in any newspaper. In spite of how we may feel about certain individuals or groups of people in our society, God seeks out all human beings to offer them the gift of his love . . . no matter how we may personally respond to them.

GROUP DISCUSSION. In what ways does the reality of God's mercy come into conflict with the world's view of "justice"?

PERSONAL REFLECTION. Identify a person or a group of people with whom you have relational difficulty. How would you respond if they committed a grievous wrong against you and our justice system granted them pardon?

Jonah's expectations of justice or fairness differed from God's responses to the Ninevites. *Read Jonah 4.*

1. Throughout the passage, what in particular causes Jonah's anger?

---

2. In what ways can you identify with Jonah's anger?

---

3. How have you seen God demonstrate the qualities Jonah mentions in verse 2?

---

4. Evidently the forty days (3:4) had already passed (v. 10) before Jonah went out to sit east of the city. Why do you think he still waited to see what would happen (v. 5)?

---

5. What does God's response in verse 6 reveal about his character?

---

6. How does the Lord use the vine as an object lesson for Jonah (vv. 6-11)?

---

7. In what ways are we sometimes more concerned about petty things (as Jonah was when the vine withered) than about those things under God's judgment?

8. In the end do you think Jonah understood God's attitude toward Nineveh? Why or why not?

---

9. In what area of your life might you be resistant to seeing things from God's perspective?

What can we do to begin seeing things more from God's perspective?

---

10. How does the way that God treats you motivate you to reach out to those who don't know him?

What have you learned from Jonah? Ask God to impress its message on your heart and help you to live out that message.

Now or Later

There are those people in our lives with whom we instantly connect and feel comfortable. Now, for a moment, consider the people in your life it is not easy to relate to. Might God be calling you to share his love with someone associated with you in that way? If so, how might you do that?

4

The Locust Invasion

Joel 1

A crisis can capture anyone's attention. But our response to a crisis can vary greatly from person to person. Some become bitter and hardened. Others quietly endure but learn nothing from the experience. A few, however, find their lives are purified, deepened and strengthened.

GROUP DISCUSSION. What is the most traumatic worldwide or national event each of the generations represented in your group has experienced? Explain.

PERSONAL REFLECTION. What has been the most traumatic event that has happened to you personally? How did God use that time of your life?

Joel is speaking to the people of Judah after a major crisis. *Read Joel 1.*

1. Describe the devastation left by the locust plague.

2. How will the plague affect the drunkards (v. 5), the priests (vv. 9, 13) and the farmers (v. 11)?

3. How would you respond to the plague if you were a member of one of these groups?

4. In verse 2, Joel asks, "Has anything like this ever happened in your days or in the days of your forefathers?" Why do you think he asks the elders this question?

5. Joel commands the elders to tell their children and grandchildren about the dramatic locust invasion (v. 3). Why is this necessary?

6. What additional commands does Joel's word from the Lord make to the people of Judah (vv. 5, 8, 11, 13-14)?

7. What significance, if any, is there to the progression in these commands?

8. Joel compares the people of Judah to a virgin mourning for her husband (v. 8). What does this metaphor say to you about the depth of relationship between God and his people?

9. How does God discipline his people today, either individually or corporately?

10. In verses 13-14 Joel calls the people to repent. How are they to demonstrate their repentance?

11. In what meaningful ways can we express our repentance today, both individually and corporately?

Ask God to show you where your inner life is in crisis and how you need to repent.

Now or Later

Repentance requires action. Describe an act of repentance from your past and the outcome. Write a prayer of thanksgiving for God's loving discipline in your life.

5

Return to the Lord!

Joel 2:1-27

In order to get to the roses, we must deal with the thorns. The teaching of Joel in the first two chapters is hard. But roses—in the form of the promises of God—lie ahead. Because he loves us, the Father disciplines us when we wander from him. The warnings we see here are God's last resort to bring his people to true repentance—a *heart* relationship rather than one of empty ritual.

GROUP DISCUSSION. How is it that Christians sometimes serve God outwardly rather than from the heart?

PERSONAL REFLECTION. Think of a time when you were just going through the motions in worship or in serving God. Talk to God about what that was like.

Joel describes the "day of the LORD" in terms of the locust invasion. *Read Joel 2:1-27.*

1. What do we learn about the day of the Lord from these verses?

_____

2. What thoughts and feelings do you have as you read this chapter?

_____

3. Do you think Joel is describing a literal locust invasion or an army invasion, which simply resembles a swarm of locusts? Explain.

_____

4. What is the significance or purpose of the first two commands in verse 1?

_____

5. What does it mean to return to the Lord "with all your heart" (vv. 12-14)?

Tell about a time in your life when you have, in some sense, returned to the Lord.

_____

6. Again Joel calls for a "holy fast . . . a sacred assembly" (Joel 1:14; 2:15-17). What is significant about the people he singles out?

7. If his people repent, what promises does the Lord make them (vv. 18-27)?

---

8. How is the day of the Lord a warning against spiritual complacency for us today?

---

9. To what three recipients does God's graciousness and compassion (v. 13) get directed (vv. 21-24), and why do you think they are chosen?

---

10. How have you experienced God's compassionate healing following an act of repentance?

Take time to "praise the name of the LORD your God" for the wonders he has worked in you (v. 26).

Now or Later

Keep a journal this week identifying the hand of the Lord in your life each day.

6

The Day of the Lord

Christians long for that great and final day when the Lord will return. But the day of the Lord will not be the same for everyone. For some it will be a day of indescribable joy and blessing. For others it will be a day of judgment and terror. The day of the Lord will come for *all* people.

GROUP DISCUSSION. In what ways do you look forward to the day of the Lord?

PERSONAL REFLECTION. What would you like to see happen in your life to be ready for the day of the Lord?

In this final section of his book, Joel looks at both the terror and the joy found on the day of the Lord. *Read Joel 2:28—3:21.*

---

1. What will be the differing experiences of the nations listed here?

2. Based on 2:28-31, what signs will precede the "coming of the great and dreadful day of the LORD"?

3. In 2:28-29 the Lord promises to pour out his Spirit. What do you think is significant about the fact that the Holy Spirit will be poured out on both male and female, young and old?

What would it feel like to experience the Spirit in this way?

4. As the dreadful day of the Lord approaches, what offer does he make (2:32)?

5. What connection is there (if any) between this offer and the promise of his Spirit?

6. Peter claimed Joel's prophecy was fulfilled on the day of Pentecost (Acts 2:17-21, 38-40). How then does Joel's promise of the Spirit and salvation apply to us?

7. The Lord commands the nations to prepare for war (3:9). How does their battle relate to the Lord's judgment (3:9-16)?

8. Joel describes the Lord as a lion, a thunderstorm, a refuge and a stronghold (3:16). What do these images reveal about the God we serve?

———————————————————————————

9. What blessings does the Lord promise his people (3:17-21)?

———————————————————————————

10. What has Joel taught you about preparing for the day of the Lord?

How does this relate to how you live every day?

Ask God what steps you need to take in order to be prepared for his return. Pray for the needed strength and commitment to follow through with these steps.

Now or Later

In his covenant promise with Abraham, God said, "I will bless those who bless you, and whoever curses you I will curse; and all peoples on earth will be blessed through you" (Genesis 12:3). How does the Lord fulfill that promise through his church today?

7

The Lord Roars from Zion

Amos 1—2

Picture this if you will. It is about the middle of the eighth century B.C. You are part of the upper-middle-class group of people who are flocking to the worship center at Bethel. The design of the building is very appealing. The choirs are polished. Several brilliant orators are at hand. It feels good to come here—uplifting music, beautiful surroundings and comforting words. There is even an opportunity to placate your conscience by bringing offerings. But wait a minute! Who is that seedy-looking character? He speaks like a shepherd; he looks like a shepherd; he even smells like a shepherd—but he sure doesn't sound like a shepherd!

GROUP DISCUSSION. Who is the most unlikely person you have ever known to speak God's truth? What credentials do you need to speak God's truth?

PERSONAL REFLECTION. How do you react when someone challenges your behavior or beliefs?

In this study we will reflect upon Amos's words to the people of Israel.
Read Amos 1—2.

1. What tone of voice do Amos's words reflect in these two chapters?

2. Consider Amos's strategy. What do you notice about the order in which he lists the nations?

3. How would you feel as the prophecy started with nations that were enemies of your nation and then moved toward nations closer to your own (1:4-5)?

4. The statement "For three sins . . . even for four" emphasizes God's patience before pronouncing judgment. What kinds of sin do the pagan nations have in common (1:3—2:3)?

5. How are Judah's sins different from those of the pagan nations (2:4-5)?

6. How might the attitude of the people change as they hear the words, "For three sins of *Israel,* even for four, I will not turn back my wrath" (2:6)?

7. Do you think it is characteristic of human nature to assume that judgment will always fall on someone else? Explain.

8. Amos cites a variety of sins of which Israel is guilty (2:6-8, 12). How would you categorize their sins?

9. Does God expect more of the Israelites (2:9-11)? Explain your response.

10. How do you see judgment happening in your culture as it did in the Israelite culture (2:13-16)?

11. How can Amos's warnings to Israel keep us from being presumptuous about our status as God's children?

---

12. In what way do you need to adjust your attitude toward other nations?

Ask God to grant you a sense of true humility.

Now or Later

What one action will you take this week to alleviate the suffering of someone who is needy, poor or oppressed?

8

Israel's Punishment

A well-known insurance company uses cartoons to advertise their product. One cartoon pictures a piano falling from an upper-story window toward an unsuspecting man below. As it speeds toward its destination, a friend politely asks: "By the way, what's the name of your insurance company?" "Acme insurance, of course," the man replies. "Why do you ask?"

Disaster often comes unexpectedly.

GROUP DISCUSSION. Why do many people have difficulty believing in God as judge?

PERSONAL REFLECTION. How does your life as a Christian look different than those you know who are not Christians?

The people of Israel were wealthy, self-centered and complacent. Little did they realize that the full weight of God's judgment was about to fall on them. *Read Amos 3.*

1. In what ways did the Israelites fall away from what God had called them to be and do (vv. 1-2)?

_____

2. It has been said, "Privilege brings responsibility." It was true for the Israelites. Give an example of how this is true for you.

_____

3. In verses 3-6 Amos asks several rhetorical questions. How would you summarize what he is trying to say in these verses?

_____

4. Why do you think the Lord does nothing without revealing his plan to the prophets (v. 7)?

_____

5. Who is invited to come and see the Lord pronounce judgment on Israel (vv. 9-10)?

_____

6. How would the Lord's judgment against Israel fit their crimes (vv. 10-11, 15)?

_____

7. What kind of salvation could these Israelites expect (v. 12)?

8. According to the law, people in danger could find refuge by grasping the horns of the altar (see 1 Kings 1:50). What situation has caused you to grasp the "horns of the altar"?

_____

9. How would being a member of the "haves" or the "have nots" affect your view of this study?

_____

10. How will you be motivated by what you have learned in this study?

Ask the Lord to give you the strength of character needed to be responsible as a person of God.

Now or Later

Consider the words of Amos. How do they apply to the people of God (the church) today?

9

Prepare to
Meet Your God!

Amos 4

In 1741 Jonathan Edwards preached his most famous sermon: "Sinners in the Hands of an Angry God." After using vivid imagery to make non-Christians feel the horror of their position, Edwards concluded: "Therefore, let every one that is out of Christ now awake and fly from the wrath to come!" God used that sermon to bring a powerful awakening to the town of Enfield, in New England.

GROUP DISCUSSION. How does the lifestyle of those who are the middle and upper classes in this society affect the poor?

PERSONAL REFLECTION. Recall a time when you wandered from God. What brought you back?

The prophet Amos preaches a similar sermon in this chapter. After warning Israel repeatedly to return to the Lord, he now declares: "Prepare to meet your God!" *Read Amos 4.*

1. How would you describe the tone of this text?

2. The area of Bashan was noted for its fat, sleek cattle. What does this say about the lifestyle of the Israelites (v. 1)?

What do you think God would point to in our culture that would be comparable to the "cows of Bashan"?

3. How does this lifestyle contrast with the judgment the Lord swears to bring upon them (vv. 2-3)?

4. Bethel and Gilgal were centers of worship for the Northern Kingdom (1 Kings 12:26-33; Hosea 4:15) What was sinful about Israel's worship at these places (vv. 4-5)?

5. What are the judgments the Lord brought on Israel (vv. 6-11)?

6. What is the purpose of the judgments that have come upon Israel?

7. Why do you think we sometimes need to be disciplined repeatedly before we will return to God?

8. Amos proclaims to Israel, "Prepare to meet your God" (v. 12). What is the purpose of this meeting?

9. The chapter closes with a brief hymn describing the God Israel would meet in judgment (v. 13). What do we learn about God from each aspect of Amos's description?

10. God's tenderness, even in the midst of judgment, is evident in the repeated words, "yet you have not returned to me" (vv. 6, 8-9, 11). How have you experienced God's grace in the midst of discipline?

Take a few minutes to worship God, using the hymn in verse 13 as the basis for your prayers.

Now or Later
How do these judgments compare to the curses of disobedience described in Deuteronomy 28:15-19?

10

Seek the Lord and Live!

Amos 5—6

Success, wealth, power, prestige—these are eagerly sought by many today. People are willing to sacrifice their marriages, their families and even their health to obtain these goals. But in the end most discover that the rewards were not worth the cost.

GROUP DISCUSSION. Why do you think people are willing to sacrifice so much to obtain the things mentioned above?

PERSONAL REFLECTION. What do you continue to do (or not do) even though it may not be good or helpful for you?

In chapters 5 and 6 Amos tells us how to avoid this tragedy in our lives. *Read Amos 5—6.*

1. Looking throughout the passage, what does Amos urge people to seek?

2. A *lament* (5:1) was a song or poem mourning someone's death. What images of death does Amos use in this lament?

3. Do you see yourself, your church or your culture in any of the statements made in 5:7 and 5:10-12? Explain.

4. What warnings of judgment does the Lord give in this chapter, and how does the Lord plead with Israel in 5:4, 6, 14-15?

5. How were the Israelites mistaken about the day of the Lord (5:18-20)?

6. Amos uses scathing language in 5:21-23. How might this prepare his audience to hear the message of 5:24?

7. If Amos were prophesying today, how would he expect us to "hate evil" and "love good" (5:15)?

8. How does Amos portray the Israelites in 6:1-6?

9. In their complacency and security, Israel failed to grieve over the ruin of their nation (6:6). What should grieve us today about our personal lives, our church and our nation?

---

10. How does the Lord promise to repay those who are complacent and proud (6:7-14)?

---

11. What changes will you make in your lifestyle as a result of this study?

Take time to pray about those things that cause you to grieve. Ask the Lord to help you seek his will in these areas.

Now or Later

On what issues, and how, will you challenge your church and community based on this study?

11

Five Visions
(Part 1)

Amos 7—8

At one time or another we've all run into a street preacher standing on a box in a park or on a street corner in a busy downtown. Sometimes they are speaking God's truth, and sometimes they seem to be yelling hysterically at anyone who will listen. It can be embarrassing to run into the latter sort of preacher, especially if we are with a friend who's a seeker.

GROUP DISCUSSION. How would you respond if you were confronted by a street preacher who warned of God's judgment?

PERSONAL REFLECTION. When have you said, or thought, "I'm just a layperson"?

Israel saw Amos as we might see a street preacher. He was a farmer who came to town and began announcing visions of judgment. In this session we will look at four of Amos's visions. *Read Amos 7—8.*

1. What characteristics do these visions have in common?

2. How can the Lord's response to Amos's prayers motivate us to pray for our nation?

3. What three visions of judgment does the Lord show Amos in chapter 7 (7:1, 4, 7)?

4. Why does the Lord relent regarding the first two visions (7:1-6)?

5. In the third vision the wall had been plumb-line-built and was being subjected to a plumb-line test. Why was this an appropriate analogy for Israel?

6. In 7:10-17, Amos undergoes his own "plumb-line" test. What temptations might he have experienced?

7. What is the source of your identity and calling (7:14-15)?

8. A basket of ripe fruit (8:1) was normally associated with the joys of summer harvest. But in this instance, it is a picture of judgment (8:2). How does Amos describe the lifestyle of those who are ripe for judgment (8:4-6)?

9. How does he describe the "harvest" they will experience (8:3-14)?

10. If we do not remain faithful to God, what kind of "famine" is inevitable (8:11-12)?

11. J. A. Motyer writes: "People who are brought near to God cannot avoid being tested and judged."* Do you agree or disagree with his statement? Explain.

---

*J. Alec Motyer, *The Day of the Lion* (Downers Grove, Ill.: InterVarsity Press, 1974), p. 160.

12. What area of your life do you think God might currently be molding?

Pray that God will use your study of Amos to mold you into the person he wants you to be.

Now or Later

Even though we may live in a country where we can freely read the Bible and worship, how does spiritual famine evidence itself among God's people? What can you do about it?

12

Five Visions
(Part 2)

Amos 9

Hope is one of the three greatest gifts. It can lift our broken spirits, strengthen our feeble bodies and transform our darkest moments into lighthearted praise.

GROUP DISCUSSION. What do you do when you are in need of hope?

PERSONAL REFLECTION. How does hope differ from wishful or "positive" thinking?

Up to this point Amos has offered little hope to Israel. But in this final chapter, as the pace toward destruction quickens, he brings his prophecy to a surprising conclusion. *Read Amos 9.*

1. This chapter is full of hope, promise and a renewed vision of God. What image does Amos use to give hope?

2. In this fifth vision Amos sees the Lord himself standing by the temple altar (v. 1). What would it be like to be standing in the temple among the people gathered there?

---

3. How would you put the description of the Lord in verses 5-6 in your own words?

---

4. The Israelites thought they were superior to other nations because God chose them and delivered them from Egypt. Why would they be shocked by verse 7 and the first part of verse 8?

---

5. What is the glimmer of hope that Amos offers the house of Jacob (vv. 8-10)?

---

6. Suddenly Israel's glimmer of hope begins to shine with intense brightness (vv. 11-15). How does Amos's final prophecy contrast with what he has said before?

---

7. After hearing all of Amos's harsh words, how would this prophecy make you feel if you were an Israelite?

8. Describe a time in your life or in the life of your church when the Lord restored what was in ruins (v. 11).

9. How do verses 11-15 help to balance the picture of God we have seen in this book?

10. How can this portrait of God give you hope even when things seem hopeless?

11. What have you appreciated most about studying Jonah, Joel and Amos?

Pray for hope in your life and in the lives of people you know who may feel hopeless.

Now or Later

What is the most important insight you have gained from these books? What might God be calling you to do in response?

Leader's Notes

Leading a Bible discussion can be an enjoyable and rewarding experience. But it can also be *scary*—especially if you've never done it before. If this is your feeling, you're in good company. When God asked Moses to lead the Israelites out of Egypt, he replied, "O Lord, please send someone else to do it"! (Ex 4:13). It was the same with Solomon, Jeremiah and Timothy, but God helped these people in spite of their weaknesses, and he will help you as well.

You don't need to be an expert on the Bible or a trained teacher to lead a Bible discussion. The idea behind these inductive studies is that the leader guides group members to discover for themselves what the Bible has to say. This method of learning will allow group members to remember much more of what is said than a lecture would.

These studies are designed to be led easily. As a matter of fact, the flow of questions through the passage from observation to interpretation to application is so natural that you may feel that the studies lead themselves. This study guide is also flexible. You can use it with a variety of groups— student, professional, neighborhood or church groups. Each study takes forty-five to sixty minutes in a group setting.

There are some important facts to know about group dynamics and encouraging discussion. The suggestions listed below should enable you to effectively and enjoyably fulfill your role as leader.

Preparing for the Study

1. Ask God to help you understand and apply the passage in your own life. Unless this happens, you will not be prepared to lead others. Pray too for the various members of the group. Ask God to open your hearts to the message of his Word and motivate you to action.

2. Read the introduction to the entire guide to get an overview of the entire book and the issues which will be explored.

3. As you begin each study, read and reread the assigned Bible passage to familiarize yourself with it.

4. This study guide is based on the New International Version of the Bible. It will help you and the group if you use this translation as the basis for your study and discussion.

5. Carefully work through each question in the study. Spend time in meditation and reflection as you consider how to respond.

6. Write your thoughts and responses in the space provided in the study guide. This will help you to express your understanding of the passage clearly.

7. It might help to have a Bible dictionary handy. Use it to look up any unfamiliar words, names or places. (For additional help on how to study a passage, see chapter five of *How To Lead a LifeGuide® Bible Study,* InterVarsity Press.)

8. Consider how you can apply the Scripture to your life. Remember that the group will follow your lead in responding to the studies. They will not go any deeper than you do.

9. Once you have finished your own study of the passage, familiarize yourself with the leader's notes for the study you are leading. These are designed to help you in several ways. First, they tell you the purpose the study guide author had in mind when writing the study. Take time to think through how the study questions work together to accomplish that purpose. Second, the notes provide you with additional background information or suggestions on group dynamics for various questions. This information can be useful when people have difficulty understanding or answering a question. Third, the leader's notes can alert you to potential problems you may encounter during the study.

10. If you wish to remind yourself of anything mentioned in the leader's notes, make a note to yourself below that question in the study.

Leading the Study

1. Begin the study on time. Open with prayer, asking God to help the group to understand and apply the passage.

2. Be sure that everyone in your group has a study guide. Encourage the group to prepare beforehand for each discussion by reading the introduction to the guide and by working through the questions in the study.

3. At the beginning of your first time together, explain that these studies are meant to be discussions, not lectures. Encourage the members of the group to participate. However, do not put pressure on those who may be hesitant to speak during the first few sessions. You may want to suggest the following guidelines to your group.

■ Stick to the topic being discussed.

■ Your responses should be based on the verses which are the focus of the discussion and not on outside authorities such as commentaries or speakers.

■ These studies focus on a particular passage of Scripture. Only rarely should you refer to other portions of the Bible. This allows for everyone to participate in in-depth study on equal ground.

■ Anything said in the group is considered confidential and will not be discussed outside the group unless specific permission is given to do so.

■ We will listen attentively to each other and provide time for each person present to talk.

■ We will pray for each other.

4. Have a group member read the introduction at the beginning of the discussion.

5. Every session begins with a group discussion question. The question or activity is meant to be used before the passage is read. The question introduces the theme of the study and encourages group members to begin to open up. Encourage as many members as possible to participate, and be ready to get the discussion going with your own response.

This section is designed to reveal where our thoughts or feelings need to be transformed by Scripture. That is why it is especially important not to read the passage before the discussion question is asked. The passage will tend to color the honest reactions people would otherwise give because they are, of course, supposed to think the way the Bible does.

You may want to supplement the group discussion question with an icebreaker to help people to get comfortable. See the community section of *Small Group Idea Book* for more ideas.

You also might want to use the personal reflection question with your group. Either allow a time of silence for people to respond individually or discuss it together.

6. Have a group member (or members if the passage is long) read aloud the passage to be studied. Then give people several minutes to read the passage again silently so that they can take it all in.

7. Question 1 will generally be an overview question designed to briefly survey the passage. Encourage the group to look at the whole passage, but try to avoid getting sidetracked by questions or issues that will be addressed later in the study.

8. As you ask the questions, keep in mind that they are designed to be used just as they are written. You may simply read them aloud. Or you may prefer to express them in your own words.

There may be times when it is appropriate to deviate from the study guide.

For example, a question may have already been answered. If so, move on to the next question. Or someone may raise an important question not covered in the guide. Take time to discuss it, but try to keep the group from going off on tangents.

9. Avoid answering your own questions. If necessary, repeat or rephrase them until they are clearly understood. Or point out something you read in the leader's notes to clarify the context or meaning. An eager group quickly becomes passive and silent if they think the leader will do most of the talking.

10. Don't be afraid of silence. People may need time to think about the question before formulating their answers.

11. Don't be content with just one answer. Ask, "What do the rest of you think?" or "Anything else?" until several people have given answers to the question.

12. Acknowledge all contributions. Try to be affirming whenever possible. Never reject an answer. If it is clearly off-base, ask, "Which verse led you to that conclusion?" or again, "What do the rest of you think?"

13. Don't expect every answer to be addressed to you, even though this will probably happen at first. As group members become more at ease, they will begin to truly interact with each other. This is one sign of healthy discussion.

14. Don't be afraid of controversy. It can be very stimulating. If you don't resolve an issue completely, don't be frustrated. Move on and keep it in mind for later. A subsequent study may solve the problem.

15. Periodically summarize what the group has said about the passage. This helps to draw together the various ideas mentioned and gives continuity to the study. But don't preach.

16. At the end of the Bible discussion you may want to allow group members a time of quiet to work on an idea under "Now or Later." Then discuss what you experienced. Or you may want to encourage group members to work on these ideas between meetings. Give an opportunity during the session for people to talk about what they are learning.

17. Conclude your time together with conversational prayer, adapting the prayer suggestion at the end of the study to your group. Ask for God's help in following through on the commitments you've made.

18. End on time.

Many more suggestions and helps are found in *How to Lead a LifeGuide*® *Bible Study.*

Components of Small Groups

A healthy small group should do more than study the Bible. There are four components to consider as you structure your time together.

Nurture. Small groups help us to grow in our knowledge and love of God. Bible study is the key to making this happen and is the foundation of your small group.

Community. Small groups are a great place to develop deep friendships with other Christians. Allow time for informal interaction before and after each study. Plan activities and games that will help you get to know each other. Spend time having fun together—going on a picnic or cooking dinner together.

Worship and prayer. Your study will be enhanced by spending time praising God together in prayer or song. Pray for each other's needs—and keep track of how God is answering prayer in your group. Ask God to help you to apply what you are learning in your study.

Outreach. Reaching out to others can be a practical way of applying what you are learning, and it will keep your group from becoming self-focused. Host a series of evangelistic discussions for your friends or neighbors. Clean up the yard of an elderly friend. Serve at a soup kitchen together, or spend a day working on a Habitat house.

Many more suggestions and helps in each of these areas are found in *Small Group Idea Book.* Information on building a small group can be found in *Small Group Leaders' Handbook* and *The Big Book on Small Groups* (both from Inter-Varsity Press). Reading through one of these books would be worth your time.

Study 1. Jonah 1—2. Jonah's Disobedience and Prayer.

Purpose: To learn that God seeks us with his grace even in times of disobedience.

Group discussion. Every study begins with an "approach" question for group discussion. These questions are important for several reasons.

First, they help a group to warm up to each other. No matter how well a group may know each other, there is always a stiffness that needs to be overcome before people will begin to talk openly. Good opening questions can help the group "break the ice."

Second, approach questions get people thinking about the topic of the study. Most people will have lots of different thoughts going on in their minds as you begin the study. These questions can help get the group's attention focused on the topic and draw them into discussion.

Third, approach questions can help us be more open to the transforming power of the Word of God. Giving honest reflection and responses to these questions before searching the Word allows the biblical narrative to speak to personal issues in our lives by the power of the Holy Spirit.

Question 2. It isn't necessary to suppose Jonah thought he could *actually* flee from the Lord. Sometimes our actions aren't logical, especially when we try to run away from God's will. Jonah simply wanted to get as far away from Nineveh as possible. It might help the group if you locate Nineveh, Joppa and Tarshish on a Bible map. If you don't have a large map of Bible lands, you may wish to photocopy a smaller one for each of the group members.

Questions 4-5. The sailors were polytheists and didn't know whose god had been offended or why. So in their fear each one cried out to his favorite god. Throughout this chapter, it is interesting to note how the pagan sailors seem far more concerned about obedience than Jonah is.

Question 6. God's grace was not only demonstrated to Jonah by providing a fish to keep him from death, but also to the sailors, who were awed by what they had witnessed. Their chief god, Baal, was a sky god. Thus, to hear that Jonah's God was the God of heaven, who made the sea and the land, and to observe how he calmed the sea would have made quite an impression.

Question 8. Most of us have been in a circumstance where we felt there was no way out. Give the group the opportunity to talk about such an experience. Was it something that they brought on themselves, or was it something out of their control?

Question 11. It is God's nature to seek those who run from him and to save those who turn to him. In Jonah's words, "Salvation comes from the LORD" (2:9). Throughout Scripture God promises to hear those who repent and turn their hearts toward him. (For example, see 1 Jn 1:9.)

Question 12. Notice that Jesus compares Jonah's experience to his own resurrection (Mt 12:38-41; Lk 11:29-30, 32). Jonah may have felt like a man "raised from the dead" once he arrived on dry land. Perhaps individuals in the group can identify "resurrection" experiences in their spiritual journeys.

Study 2. Jonah 3. Jonah's Obedience.

Purpose: To learn about genuine repentance from both Jonah and the Ninevites.

Group discussion. Karl Menninger's book *Whatever Became of Sin?* may well indicate that the concept of repentance is no longer understood well in Western culture. Discuss what that might mean for the people of God in your country. What other cultures are represented in your group? How well are obedience and repentance understood in those cultures?

Question 1. Try to see the humor as well as the seriousness in verses 1-2. After all that Jonah had experienced, these words would have been the Lord's way of saying: "*Now* are you willing to obey me?" Jonah's response this time was an unhesitating "*Yes, Sir!*"

Question 3. Help the group to focus on both Assyria's might (they were considered very difficult to overthrow; their empire lasted three hundred years) and their brutality (what would they do to someone like Jonah who proclaimed their destruction?). Assyria was known for its cruel and vicious treatment of those whom they conquered. Are there any present-day parallels?

Verse 3 mentions, "Now Nineveh was a very important city—a visit required three days." Modern archaeology has shown that the inner wall had a length of almost eight miles. Still, this is a lot smaller than a three-day journey. It is probable that Jonah was referring to greater Nineveh, the area that included the entire administrative district.

Questions 4-5. The book of Jonah was probably written during the period of Assyrian weakness between the death of Adad-nirari III (793-753 B.C.) and the beginning of the reign of Tiglath-pileser III in 745 B.C. During this period Assyria was in a life-and-death struggle with tribes to the north and feared for its survival. This may help to account for the fact that the people so readily accepted Jonah's message, although this explanation is not meant to detract from the miraculous nature of what happened.

Question 7. Look at the view of God expressed by their actions as well as by their words.

The Ninevites were polytheists, but their national god was Ashur. Yet behind most polytheistic religions lies a belief in a supreme god capable of exerting his will over all others. We aren't told whether the Ninevites rejected their other deities, but it is clear that they recognized the existence and power of the Supreme God.

Questions 9-10. These questions might cause some members of the group to feel uncomfortable. You might put them at ease if you mention that they don't have to reveal any deep, dark secrets but simply identify one area where they need or desire to change. After all, as Christians we are continually in the process of change as we become more like Jesus Christ.

Study 3. Jonah 4. Jonah's Anger.

Purpose: To realize that God's perspective of justice and mercy is not always the same as the world's view.

Question 1. Some possible responses may include: (1) God's compassion and graciousness, (2) God's slowness to anger and abundant love, (3) God's willingness to not send destruction, (4) the destruction of the vine which had provided Jonah shade from the hot sun.

Question 2. Jonah was on an emotional roller coaster in this chapter. Ask participants if they have experienced these kinds of changeable feelings in their own relationship with God. Note that God handles Jonah's anger with compassion and graciousness as well. Help the group to see some of the humor in this chapter. Do you think God has a sense of humor?

Question 4. In any narrative portion of Scripture we need to use our imaginations in order to get the full effect of what is taking place. In verse 5 it is helpful to imagine Jonah's mood. The Lord had already decided not to destroy Nineveh—and Jonah knew this. Therefore, his actions are simply stubborn and childish. He goes outside the city to pout and to wait for something he wishes would happen but which he knows will not.

Question 5. In many ways Jonah's reactions are both humorous and pathetic. Even so, God provides relief from the sun, another sign of his graciousness and compassion.

Question 6. Jonah would have been happy about Nineveh's destruction, but he wanted to die because of the death of a silly vine. Jonah was not wrong to feel sad about the vine—although his reaction was a bit extreme! Likewise, there's nothing wrong with our being concerned about the smaller matters of life. But like Jonah we sometimes have a misplaced sense of values. We sometimes care more about a wrecked automobile or a broken television than we do about those who die daily without food or without Christ. Once again we see the compassion and graciousness of God in the gentle object lesson the Lord uses to let Jonah know how mixed up his values have become.

Question 9. Help the group to think of ways we can reorient our thoughts and feelings so that we can see things from God's perspective. Consider what Scripture teaches about how God seeks the lost, for example, the parables of the lost sheep, the lost coin and the lost son (Lk 15:3-32).

Question 10. If you have time, you may wish to discuss practical ways of reaching out to people who don't know Christ. For example, you could begin praying for lost friends or start a seeker Bible study. Discuss how, in small ways, each day our actions and words can make the gospel more attractive to people.

Study 4. Joel 1. The Locust Invasion.

Purpose: To realize that true repentance requires action.

Questions 1-2. These questions overlap somewhat, moving from a general overview of the devastation to some of its specific effects on the people in the land.

Witnesses of similar plagues in the 1930s tell of dark clouds of locusts cutting off the sunlight, stopping trains on the tracks and wiping out entire fields overnight. This would have a devastating effect on an agrarian society. "The supplies of wine for the wealthy and the rich would be cut off by the plague. The farmers would no longer be able to 'sit under one's vine and fig tree,' the sign of prosperity" (Derward Deere, *The Wycliffe Bible Commentary,* ed. Charles F. Pfeiffer [Chicago: Moody Press, 1962], p. 821).

The cessation of daily sacrifice was a great calamity for the people of God. This was the sign of God's covenant relationship. Sacrifices had been offered for hundreds of years (since the time of Abraham) and provided a tremendous sense of security. A serious breach had occurred in God's covenant relationship with his people.

Question 3. Some of the human responses within the grieving process include shock and denial, anger, depression (or despair), guilt and bargaining, and finally acceptance.

Question 4. Joel seems to be saying that this is no ordinary event. Rather, it is so extraordinary that the people should recognize it as God's judgment. It is God's way of getting their attention and disciplining them for their sin. See Deuteronomy 28:15, 38, which refers to a specific curse of disobedience.

Question 5. This kind of oral tradition ("tell it to your children, and let your children tell it to their children") is common in many cultures. When Alex Haley was doing research in Africa for *Roots,* he spoke to a local "griot" who narrated oral history for over three days without repeating himself, echoing what Haley had heard over the many years of his boyhood! Such history warned the younger generations against repeating the mistakes of the past.

Question 9. This question cannot be answered from the text, but it is still important. Whenever we are dealing with Old Testament passages that have no *direct* application to us today, we must look for *parallels* between our situation and theirs. This question looks for such parallels between God's disciplining the people of Judah and his disciplining his people today. Possible references for further discussion include Proverbs 3:11-12, 1 Peter 1:6-7 and Hebrews 12:7-11.

Question 10. Sackcloth (v. 13) was a garment of camel or goat's hair wrapped around the loins, typically signifying mourning. Evidence indicates that it also could have looked like a corn sack with openings for the head, arms and legs. Fasting (v. 14) was also associated with mourning (see 2 Sam 12:16).

Study 5. Joel 2:1-27. Return to the Lord!

Purpose: To realize that true repentance is a matter of the heart and results in blessing.

Question 3. Different opinions exist regarding the interpretation of chapter 2. Some commentators view it as a continuation of the description of the locust invasion in chapter 1. Others suggest it describes a future army which is to attack Israel on the day of the Lord. Notice, however, that the locust invasion in chapter 1 has passed, while the invasion in chapter 2 will occur in the future (v. 2).

Question 4. Joel calls on the people to blow the trumpet to announce the day of the Lord. The trumpet of that day was made from a ram's horn and was used to call people to worship, to battle or (as in this case) to warn them of imminent danger.

Question 5. Notice that hope is offered if the people will return to the Lord with all their *heart* (v. 12). In Hebrew, *heart* denotes the center of life, "the locus of emotions, personality, intellect, sensibility and will" (*Wycliffe Bible Commentary*, p. 823).

Rending one's garments (v. 13) was a sign of mourning, grief or displeasure (see Acts 14:14).

Question 6. Fasting and gathering for a sacred assembly occurs elsewhere in the Old Testament. For example, when Jehoshaphat became afraid at the advance of an army from Edom, he "resolved to inquire of the LORD, and he proclaimed a fast for all Judah. The people of Judah came together to seek help from the LORD" (2 Chron 20:3-4).

The people Joel singles out are from every age group (elders and children). Those who normally would rejoice (bride and bridegroom) are now called to fast and to join in the solemn mood (v. 16). There is also a note of urgency—even the bride and bridegroom are not to wait for the wedding ceremony. Everyone must come immediately!

Question 7. Notice that many of these promises reverse the devastation brought on by the locust plague (see chapter 1).

Question 8. Traditionally the Hebrews viewed the "day of the Lord" as a time when his faithful followers would be blessed and his enemies punished. Joel, however, describes it as a day of destruction, darkness and gloom.

Although there will be only one final day of the Lord, there are many events throughout history that are manifestations of God's judgment and therefore resemble the day of the Lord. The locust invasion in chapter 1 and the subsequent invasion in chapter 2 fall into this category.

What events of our day warn against spiritual complacency?

Study 6. Joel 2:28—3:21. The Day of the Lord.

Purpose: To discover why people's experience of the day of the Lord will vary.

Question 2. Joel states that the signs will occur both in heaven ("the sun will be turned to darkness and the moon to blood") and on earth ("blood and fire and billows of smoke"). The blood, fire and smoke may be the result of warfare.

Question 3. Under the Old Covenant the Spirit was given to select individuals for specific tasks (see Num 11:24-30). But according to Joel, a day would come when no distinction would be made on the basis of race, sex, age, nationality or social position. All the people of God would receive his Spirit with all the various gifts. This would, no doubt, bring a deep sense of fulfillment and joy to believers and judgment to nonbelievers.

Question 5. Joel isn't clear about the relationship between the offer of salvation (2:32) and the promise of the Spirit (2:28-29), although they obviously seem to be related. Peter, however, clearly states that those who receive salvation also receive the Spirit (Acts 2:38-39).

Question 6. We may view this as a prophecy that *has* been fulfilled, *is* being fulfilled in the church today, and *will* be fulfilled in that great and final Day of the Lord.

Question 7. The Lord states that he "will enter into judgment against them" in the Valley of Jehoshaphat (v. 2). Although there was a Valley of Jehoshaphat in the fourth century A.D., there is no evidence that there was literally such a place in Joel's day. *Jehoshaphat* means "the Lord judges." The point is that all the nations will be gathered together for judgment.

The battle itself is an expression of the Lord's judgment. Joel isn't clear about whether the nations are destroying each other in battle or whether their destruction is a result of divine intervention. Either way, it is clear that the blood of the nations will flow freely because of God's judgment (see Rev 14:14-20).

Now or Later. In his covenant promise with Abraham, God said, "I will bless those who bless you, and whoever curses you I will curse; and all peoples on earth will be blessed through you" (Gen 12:3). God continues to bless the nations through his people. Judgment comes against those who hinder that work through God's people. God continues to be faithful to his covenant children. (See Acts 3:25-26.)

Study 7. Amos 1—2. The Lord Roars from Zion.
Purpose: To consider why the Lord's wrath was against Israel and its enemies.

Question 1. Amos was a shepherd. As a shepherd he would have had a strong voice. The text reflects a wide range of emotions, but as we will later see, the purpose for warning and judgment is to bring God's people back into relationship with him.

Questions 2-3. Amos begins by prophesying against the pagan nations surrounding Israel. Damascus, Gaza, Tyre, Edom, Ammon and Moab all represented enemies of Israel. We may imagine the people smugly agreeing with him, since most of these countries represented enemies and were threats at one time or another.

Questions 5-6. Next, he turns to the southern kingdom of Judah. The division between Israel and Judah had caused deep wounds, which were never completely healed, and so Joel's prophecy against Judah would probably be welcomed by those in Israel. But as the masterful preacher turns and shouts, "For three sins of *Israel*, even for four, I will not turn back my wrath" (2:6), the people would be caught in what has been described as Amos's "coil of condemnation."

Question 8. Think of categories such as oppression, injustice, immorality and so on.

Question 9. This is the first time Amos has mentioned "the law of the LORD" and "his decrees." The Lord judges people according to the light he has given them.

In verse 7 Amos says, "Father and son use the same girl and so profane my holy name." Evidently, the Israelites had adopted some of the practices of the Canaanite fertility religions and as a result had temple prostitutes. However, it is also possible that Amos is speaking against incest.

In verse 8 Amos mentions: "They lie down beside every altar on *garments taken in pledge.*" This was a violation of the Jewish law which stated, "If you take your neighbor's cloak as a pledge, return it to him by sunset, because his cloak is the only covering he has for his body. What else will he sleep in?" (Ex 22:26-27).

Nazirites (v. 12) were not to cut their hair or drink wine. They were living reminders to Israel of being set apart for God.

Questions 10-11. Between questions 10 and 11, you might ask the group to compare the lifestyle in the Western world to the lifestyle of those Amos addressed, and ask what effects that lifestyle has on others.

If you choose to discuss this, you might mention the following. According to Arthur Simon, author of *Breaking Bread with the Hungry*, "One out of eighteen people in the world live in the U.S. That one eighteenth of the world's population, it so happens, gathers 35% of the world's income, 20% of humanity (basically Europe and America), controls 80% of the world's resources, which leaves 80% of the world's population to divide the remaining fraction of the world's resources" ([Minneapolis: Augsburg, 1971], p. 23). The book *Rich Christians in an Age of Hunger* by Ronald Sider would be an excellent resource for discussing this topic.

Study 8. Amos 3. Israel's Punishment.

Purpose: To understand that greater privileges bring greater responsibility—and the possibility of greater judgment.

Questions 1-2. You may wish to have the group discuss the difference

between election and divine favoritism. It is important to remember that these people were originally "chosen" to be a blessing to all nations.
Question 3. Amos speaks of visible signs to warn the people. When the lion roars, the prey will be attacked; when the trumpet sounds, the people prepare for war; when the Lord speaks, the people have been warned.
Question 4. God has always provided his people with myriad opportunities of escape from forthcoming judgment by getting his message across through his chosen "mouthpieces."
Question 7. Many times shepherds saw the meager remains of one of their animals after it had been devoured by a predator. Amos uses this experience to portray the meager remains of God's chosen people.
"Those who sit . . . on the edge of their beds and . . . on their couches" (v. 12) refers to the idle luxury of the rich.
Question 8. In verse 14 Amos is saying that people will come to grasp the horns of the altar and will find nothing to grab! This is a vivid way of saying that there will be no refuge from the Lord's judgment because of the severity of Israel's sins.
One of Israel's sins involved incorporating elements of paganism into their worship, especially by setting up a worship site in Bethel (v. 14).

Study 9. Amos 4. Prepare to Meet Your God!
Purpose: To see how God disciplines us in order to bring us back to him.
Question 1. The repetition of Amos's sermon establishes a theme in this text: "Yet you did not return to me."
Question 2. According to J. A. Motyer, women were "the final guardians of morals, fashions, and standards." By using women as the example here, Amos has isolated the heartbeat of Israel's society (*The Message of Amos* [Downers Grove, Ill.: InterVarsity Press, 1974], p. 93).
Question 3. In verse 2 the statement "The Sovereign LORD has sworn by his holiness" adds tremendous weight to the message which follows. If Israel continues in sin, certain consequences are inevitable.
Question 4. Jeroboam I, the first king of the Northern Kingdom, broke the laws of Moses by establishing worship centers at Bethel and Dan. He was concerned that his subjects would go to Jerusalem and be won back to David's house. He later set up golden bulls in the sanctuaries, thus opening the door for the influence of Baal worship. Priests refused to serve at these new altars, so Jeroboam hired his own priests with little concern for their qualifications.
The reign of Jeroboam II, a contemporary of Amos (785-744 B.C.), was

marked with the same kind of idolatry as his predecessor. By this time worship was going on not only at Bethel and Dan but also at subsidiary temples at Gilgal and Beersheba.

Question 7. Help the group to notice the repetition of the phrase "yet you have not returned to me" (vv. 6, 8-11). God's judgments were not simply punishment for sin but were designed to bring the people back to him. Unfortunately, they refused to respond.

Question 9. Be sure to view this hymn in the context of God's threat of judgment. How might this description of God strike fear in the hearts of the people?

Study 10. Amos 5—6. Seek the Lord and Live!
Purpose: To see the grief of a just God as he urges his people to seek him.

Question 2. God had promised Abraham that his descendants would be as numerous as the stars in the sky (Gen 15:5). But Amos declares that Israel will be like a virgin who died childless. This would be a shocking statement to the Israelites.

Question 3. Get the group to think about how we do these things individually and corporately in our actions and non-action.

Question 5. Because they assumed they had special privilege, the Israelites looked forward to the day of the Lord. How might Christians make the same mistake about the return of Christ?

Question 7. This should provide an interesting discussion on what Christians of various persuasions and backgrounds see as important issues.

Question 8. You may wish to ask the group to note the specific terms used in these verses.

The word *roll* (5:24) derives from the same Hebrew word as *Gilgal* (5:5). Gilgal was the place where the Israelites were circumcised after entering the Promised Land, the place where the Lord "rolled away the reproach of Egypt" from them (Josh 5:9). Amos declares that justice should now roll like a river in Israel rather than the empty religion of Gilgal.

Question 10. Notice that Israel is condemned in 6:6 not for what they had done but for what they had *failed* to do. This is one of the serious problems that results from being complacent (6:1) about our Christian lives.

Study 11. Amos 7—8. Five Visions (Part 1).
Purpose: To realize that failure to respond to God's Word results in judgment and leads to an inability to hear God's Word.

Question 3. The group should be able to quickly identify the visions of locusts (vv. 1-2), fire (v. 4) and plumb line (vv. 7-9). After they have identified these visions, ask them to describe the first two. The third vision will be discussed more fully in question 5.

You may wish to point out one important item to the group. In the one hundred verses in Amos 1—6, the title "the Sovereign LORD" (RSV "the Lord GOD") is used only nine times. However, in the last three chapters the title is used eleven times in only forty-six verses. Amos is stressing the fact that the Sovereign Lord has the power to carry out his threats and promises.

Question 4. Some members of the group may wonder how a God who never changes could relent. It isn't necessary to get into a detailed theological discussion on the nature of God. It is sufficient to point out that Scripture affirms that God responds to our prayers and that they seem to have a real effect on the outcome of events. For other examples, you might mention Genesis 18:22-33, where Abraham intercedes for Sodom and Gomorrah, and Exodus 32:9-14, where Moses intercedes for Israel.

Question 5. If anyone in the group has used a plumb line, ask them to explain what it is and what it's used for. If no one has had this experience, you might explain that a plumb line is a line with a weight attached at the end. It is used for determining whether a structure is truly vertical.

Question 8. Here again we see the language of a farmer/shepherd addressing an agrarian people. Harvest was very important to the Hebrew people, as it is to any culture. Three seasons of harvest occurred during the year in Palestine: the barley harvest (April-May), the wheat harvest (June-July) and the ingathering of the fruits in the fall. This image is used by Amos to emphasize the abundance of sin among God's people.

Question 9. This question covers a lot of verses, so don't feel that you must cover every detail in every verse. Instead, encourage the group to summarize the judgments Israel will experience.

Dan (v. 14) was one of the locations for an idolatrous calf set up by Jeroboam to maintain political control in the Northern Kingdom (1 Kings 12:28-30). The worship of the goddess Ashima, prevalent among foreign settlers in Samaria, was also creeping into the religion of God's people. Evidently these changes were viewed as simply characteristics of the times with no harm intended to the faith. But the Lord viewed them as idolatrous.

Now or Later. In the parable of the sower (Mt 13) Jesus warns that while those who respond to his message will be given more, those who fail to respond will lose their opportunity to respond. In other words, we can become spiritually calloused and insensitive if we fail to respond to the light that is given to us. This is a great danger in the church today.

Study 12. Amos 9. Five Visions (Part 2).

Purpose: To see that hope, not judgment, is God's final word to Israel and to us.

Question 2. Unfortunately, older versions of the NIV have a different translation of verse 1 than that found in newer versions. The older version says:
"Strike the tops of the pillars so that the thresholds shake. *Cut off the heads* of
the people." The new version says: "Strike the tops of the pillars so that the
thresholds shake. *Bring them down on the heads* of the people." The latter version gives a much better picture of what happens when the temple collapses.

The temple mentioned in verse 1 is probably not the temple in Jerusalem
but rather symbolizes the religion of the Northern Kingdom. The vision
emphasizes that idolatry leads to judgment.

Question 4. Cush (v. 7) occupied the territory south of Egypt and was the
"Ethiopia" of classical writers. Evidently it was considered an insignificant
nation in the ancient Near East. The Israelites would be shocked to learn that
they were no better than the Cushites. They would also be shocked to learn
that the Lord had guided the migration of the Philistines and the Arameans,
just as he had led Israel from Egypt. The exodus was the primary redemptive
event in Israel's history, and they considered it (and themselves) unique.

Questions 5-6. After so many prophecies of doom, Amos's words in verses 8-
15 seem out of place to some scholars. However, Amos does not offer hope to
Israel as a whole but rather to the faithful remnant within the nation (vv. 9-10).

Question 8. Since this is a very personal question, you might encourage the
group to share by first giving an example from your life. A further reference to
use might be Romans 8:28.

Question 11. Be sure to leave enough time for this question, since it allows
the group to reflect on what they have learned from these three prophetic
books.

*Doug Haugen is the director of Lutheran Men in Mission, the men's ministry of the
Evangelical Lutheran Church in America, and a freelance author. Doris Haugen is
the director of student services for the division of adult and continuing education
at Judson College in Elgin, Illinois.*